Warm from the Thicket

Elisabeth A. King

Warm from the Thicket. Copyright © 2018 Elisabeth A. King. Produced and printed by Stillwater River Publications. All rights reserved. Written and produced in the United States of America.

This book may not be reproduced or sold in any form without the expressed, written permission of the author and publisher.

Visit our website at www.StillwaterPress.com for more information.

First Stillwater River Publications Edition

Library of Congress Control Number: 201864210

ISBN-10: 1-946-30091-8
ISBN-13: 978-1-946-30091-1

1 2 3 4 5 6 7 8 9 10

Written by Elisabeth A. King
Photography by Elisabeth A. King
Published by Stillwater River Publications, Pawtucket, RI, USA.

Publisher's Cataloging-In-Publication Data
(Prepared by The Donohue Group, Inc.)

Names: King, Elisabeth A., author, photographer.
Title: Warm from the thicket / Elisabeth A. King ; [photography by Elisabeth A. King].
Description: First Stillwater River Publications edition. | Pawtucket, RI, USA : Stillwater River Publications, [2018]
Identifiers: ISBN 9781946300911 | ISBN 1946300918
Subjects: LCSH: King, Elisabeth A.--Family--Poetry. | Mothers--Death--Psychological aspects--Poetry. | Mother and child--Poetry. | Grief--Poetry.
Classification: LCC PS3611.I57596 W37 2018 | DDC 811/.6--dc23

The views and opinions expressed in this book are solely those of the author and do not necessarily reflect the views and opinions of the publisher.

Dedication

For my mother who gave me words and wildflowers,

red winged blackbirds and ocean in my soul.

For my beloved mother who taught me compassion and perspective and how to tilt my head and see a different story.

For you, my mother, I offer this…

What I have and who I am is because of who you were.

tiny fingers,

let your first memories

be of me as you

wash through the infancy of a

stranger's hands and

the arms that

held your insecurity.

let me be what you remember first

the way your eyes reveled equal to

christmas tree shining.

let those memories begin as

open mouth kisses and

tiny hands on my face.

what dreams begin as falling asleep

my heart against yours

beating in tandem.

let this be our genesis as

you call me, "mama"

and

i claim you as my own.

      i am here
before frozen root and
solid ground where

snow comes

heavy and thick

to rally it's fortress

strong.

the first fall of
the new year.

even the

sharpest of days

and

weary unrest

can be

softly mended by

moonlight

and

baby kisses.

the earth settles and

brings me back to

rooted sound of

wispy breeze through

tall red oaks.

lavender candles and

early evening rain,

mourning dove noise and

butterfly bush.

folding

blue

checkered

dish clothes and

remembering her hand in mine.

these things remain

in the august

you

never

breathed.

having a mind filled with words

is messy enough

without them all talking at once.

like starving children trapped in a

shadow boxed shadow

and

pushing to get out

i am forever

    tripping

        over

            each

                syllable.

i am the daughter of a

weary road of

earth dirt and

weathered stones from

the ebb and flow of bare feet in the river.

i am the residue of dust that lingers the tops of

unopened books in small abandoned libraries where

we once sat on

leather chairs so you could be quiet and still and

listen to the rain through the screen.

i am starlight and mossy rock,

sunlight through tall, thin branches.

i am the trail you follow when

the moon rises full and your steps are

sacred and undecided

i am.

i am.

i am.

here.

your curls,

filled with

fresh spring air

strangle

my lungs

as i

inhale

your breath

to remember.

new england spring
(reminiscent of april snow)

the snow came fast and

early

(spring dug into the roots of the

daffodil and crocus.

confused.

hiding)

while impossible winds off the atlantic

swirled the frozen air around

the magnolia

making it almost impossible to tell the difference

between the fat flakes floating and the

blossoms which just became.

i tend to drift away slowly, at first, but present just the same.

my body, restless but too numb

to fall where the snow has become a

drift of its own mind, kind, spirit.

cold hands of winter calling the

letters of my name to follow your breath into the air.

I drift away.

like a sharp shard of lightning streaming through the

half moon spring

and

hell beating on my hurried breathing

i am a memory flashing

across the night.

beautiful mourning, I feel you on my neck

and

in my veins.

only to find you sleeping

I close your eyes with my

hands.

i shall be still.

quiet and

just a whisper.

    centering.

    peace.

    shhhh.

let me rest my head

on your chest.

let me hear your

heartbeat breathing its

lullaby as i trace this moment

of stillness

quiet and just whisper.

    you breathe.

cardinal in the koi pond

water lilies float past the

mallards

who have found

nest in nearby banks.

your tiny hand grips mine

tightly as we sneak past

snapping turtles

relentlessly sunning

on this

thursday afternoon

in the park.

i stumbled at first not knowing where to step.

she had been watching for days now and finally her perch was on the earth and

we both hesitated to share in the silence.

i stepped forward

(in retrospect, i probably should have slipped out of my clogs)

and advanced with quiet steps towards what i knew would change my perspective.

she did not fly but more so sprang across the new grass and into the side yard.

i was thankful for the moment in where i felt connected to her wings, her eyes

and red breast beating.

the house was quiet and the coffee was rich in fragrant memories of lessons on birds.

i sat on the old wooden chair by the window to the side yard

where the cherry blossoms are beginning to spring forward and

it's branches entangling each other like ancient arms reaching across for one last embrace.

and there she nestled among the twisted twigs

the same robin, the same reason i became drawn towards the strange tranquility that

met me upon my first stumble.

we remained fixed in our positions.

she on her perch and i on my chair.

nothing but the thin window glass between us.

i sipped my coffee.

remembering another time where i held another's hand and

rejoiced in the first sign of a new season.

inhale. exhale.

she flew away.

(for B.)

sun tipping on the springboard of summer

we go to the ocean for

air and breath.

horseshoe crab rooted in the

tide low with

smooth stones,

gold glittering in the

second hand sun.

i hold you on my hip and

walk slowly

wanting to hunt sea glass but more

desperately

wanting to watch your face,

your eyes witnessing the

surf

and sea

in your curls caressing the salt that

settles on your lips and on your lashes.

our first steps in the atlantic.

it is the end of may.

she persists in relinquishing her

childhood and

daisies and

pink with glitter and glue.

stuff of play swings,

mother, may i

and walking in my shoes.

i am tethered here while she

floats away

drifts to a place that

i am not

where she will gather no moss or

wilt from the sun.

evening song and eventide.

my girl

my breath

my loss.

first frost of sunday
the day of your death
your frozen breath
on the last blades of grass
and
orange chrysanthemums.
your grave must be
cold
                            as stone usually is
                            on the first frost of sunday.

i think i shall die in october when the ground is not yet frozen and the leaves are gasping for life. you will be reminded by the sugar maple that i am but ashes on your antique dresser and salty sea glass from a long holiday weekend.

i think i shall die in october when the grass stops growing and sunset starts rising. you will be reminded by the canadian geese that sweep past your window and bittersweet berries that collide with the lilac bush in the back of the back yard.

i think i shall die in october when you have the winter to harness your mourning. you will be reminded by the first snow fall and frost tipped gardens that you planted as i watched. the smell of fire place smoke still in your hair.

i think i shall die in october when the snowdrops begin to bloom and spring has gained her grace. you will be reminded by the daffodils and the first morning you open your windows to hear the birds in the pines and the wind chiming gently.

i think i shall die in october when the ocean is calling you to come. you will be reminded by the changing tides and faint fog horn sound, of sweet peas and blackberries. the fireflies will flick and flitter like the fairies we tried to catch.

i think i shall die in october while the montauk daisies are still bloomed and there is still time to plant for the forthcoming season of the day after the next.

in the calm of an autumn evening

i stop and feel my skin grow cold in

the bitterness of pre-winter silence.

please be patient.

my summer rages on.

i keep them for you,

you know.

these thoughts

these oddities of a

twisted soul entwined

with an overwrought

sense of

obligation

where you stand

waiting on

another

parallel space which is

too high to touch

and

too far to fall

if i let go.

orlando passing
(june 12, 2016)

she is quiet tonight

in her corner of the study

dimly lit

with the windows open.

the pushy atlantic shore breeze

presses through, engulfing

the long white curtains

that whip at

her bare legs.

hands trembling for her

faith,

for grief,

for grace and

humanity.

unseasonably cool for

a midnight in june

unseasonably cruel forever.

she pulls for the knitted blanket

but even then

cannot warm her fear.

what is the sense of it all

the noise

the buzz

the endless, endless,

endless

talking.

are you even listening?

what?

i can't even hear you over it all.

so for now

i'll just

close my eyes and

sink into my

rooted silence.

the only place for peace.

she came as if summoned by september and

it's breeze,

so soft and heavy

and

perched herself

alone among the lavender leaves.

flitting remembrances

cause me to invite her in so

she would never leave but teach me

(perhaps)

how to be so eloquent with my own wings.

memories darting around like interruptions when

only for a moment

(a life time)

you close your eyes

and search again to scan until

refocused.

she disappears.

the humidity made the windows stick

and the screaming had already started.

her little hands tinkling at the high notes on the piano so only she could hear

their intermittent periods like a morse code for just one night of peace.

by now, the neighbors have gathered on their porches and front stairs to

hear the latest from the grownups who pounded around and threw their bleeding

hearts at one another through a constant rattle of senseless sentences and words

that left bullet hole evidence in the kitchen walls.

one by one by one

she slid from room to room

closing each window as she went.

to keep the silence out or the arguing in,

she wasn't sure.

no kind soul ever asked or even thought to knock as if

what they were hearing was a

way of life

they had become accustomed to witnessing.

the seven o'clock show that stank of too much beer and another home cooked meal gone wrong.

And the food was now cold.

no one ever came to help close the windows

especially on a humid night when there was no chance for the tiny hands

closing

and locking

each and every one.

(for H.K.)

she flutters about

and darts in random direction.

her wings are new and ready to

float her far away from

childhood

as she stands before the

great door

and

top step.

she clings to the last single second

and

pushes through.

many times i thought of poisoning it.

the sunday night falls and the

soft, warm wave of a new

pot of coffee comes sauntering up the stairs

to remind me that

he would be here another week.

always on a sunday and then

absently leave it

black and cold

on the kitchen counter to grow more

strong and sturdy

each day until

it was

finally finished

by the next saturday morning.

each time

i knew he was staying.

and prayed that the pot would break.

She and the sun were barely awake when she heard the gentle rattle of Opa's car on the road. He had come for her and held her hand. Tightly.

"Don't look back," he told her.

She didn't.

It would be almost a year before she saw her mother again.

in flashes, you come,

unexpected

heat lightning

across an innocent

late summer sky.

a flash of mourning

and of

warning this child to

reach from her wreckage

and climb inside.

Safe. Shelter. Harbor.

you come across as lightning

igniting my weathervane

in silent

reprimand.

i guess you could call it

maintaining.

that place where you are altogether

and put together in all the right places.

your heart beating in time with your

soul so you can find that high medium of

still waters and calm ocean.

ebb and flow making sensible connections to

your movement and balance.

maintaining

the small space you have dug out of and

weeded.

where the hole is still there and the

roots have been pulled and tossed

disregarded for

hope and clinging to something real

and attainable.

i am

maintaining

and it is like i am cut in half,

living in both places

lending myself to the now and what was

ever to come before.

my mother would take me apple picking on

rainy days in autumn.

with nothing in her pockets except for the

termination letter and a receipt of payment

we would drive long winding roads.

the unseen.

the unheard.

we would climb craggy walls

in hopes that the

harvest orchard owner would not be there

instead,

warming himself by a fire

at a nearby residence that

we could not see.

we would only take a few.

stolen if not borrowed

and hold them tight on the car ride home.

our brown bags tearing

…the makings of

paper and rain.

she would reach over

and hold my hand and

i was thankful for the wet grass on my shoes.

secrets

held

within

six

feet

of

my

grasp.

the

small

box

of

ashes

preserves

all

the

answers

she had told me.

warned me that this day would arrive but never did I think it would be without the

beating of chest or sobs of grief escaping like demons from corners of hell that go without notice.

it came almost on schedule.

a friday so we would have the weekend to familiarize ourselves with this new construct of family.

she told me it was going to happen and she would be grateful for how it was done.

the emergency medical team swarmed upon her bed, darting about like confused moths to a familiar flame. I stood ten feet away, afraid to get drawn in.

my answer was slow, deliberate, "no."

i fingered through her documents with enough certainty that the moths recoiled and the flame embedded its embers into eternity.

1947 ended all too abruptly in a snowstorm that birthed my mother on the first day of the new year. Barbara Ann was born to Erika and Ralph Bergstrom on January 1, 1948. A day documented by clinks of champagne glasses, new motives and lofty resolutions. Flashes of visions and forecasts as to what this new child would bring to her parent's already unsteady marriage. She would be the first child to Ralph but second to her mother. For Erika, her "first" always came first and she held onto him as a symbolic gesture of her better decisions and younger, more vivid days of being an independent woman. Ralph was her second life and so was Barbara. And none of it ever made complete sense to her.

i

will

whisper

this

sad

symphony

into

the

mad,

delirious sea.

it falls on a tuesday this year,

where the ground is not quite as solid as

winter but still

tender as the

october leaves fall from the

maple to the

grave of my mother who once

planted tiger lilies in the summer sun

and sipped

chamomile tea out of an

earthenware mug she

inherited from

an old cupboard

rooted in the

cottage on the

lake side.

tuesday will mark three years

and the mug

now holds geraniums.

she stopped all the clocks at

seven thirty

and silenced their pendulums

from taking any more

time away

before she was ready to

say

goodbye.

in the void of movement

back and forth

the sway of copper and numbers

she sat

half waiting for the chimes

that would never fill

the silence.

the silence

of time run out of

time.

it was summer the last time

you loved me

when we walked in

zigzag patterns along the

seaside.

our feet bare to the late day

sand and messenger bags

around our shoulders

hunting for weathered

sea glass.

a long term memory of a

day once celebrated.

your hair in ringlets around your

neck like Oma from the salty mist

that settled on our shoulders.

we walked the seaside

you and i

the last day you loved me.

swirling in rebellion of turmoil and solace she reaches the door that claims, "welcome all." does she dare? does she touch? and he meets her there.
through the door she falls into a place where she could see the moon.
a place where she could become the sun.
he calls her further with dark claws retracting, projecting the stars and blinding her eyes.
swirling in rebellion of turmoil and quiet she reaches the door that claims, "welcome all."
call me. call me. bring the light. the sun must shine. please. bring the light.
now bursting through, the door is open, swaying closed. still time to revolve the moon and stars but she clings to the dark and the door that says. "welcome all."
I Am the sun. I Am the light that hazes your shadow. come. will you come and swirl into solace where light burns your darkness. I Am here.
swirling in rebellion of turmoil and spirit she reaches the door that claims, "welcome all."

the

sweet

smell

of

hay field

fresh

turns

my

face

toward

the

field

and

glancing,

i

find

you

there

the thought never occurred to me that i would arrive and enter so lightly.

the hum of the lights and smell of disinfectant would surely halt my veins as i glided past room upon room upon room.

upwell of fast panic and heavy, furious eye contact avoided.

we entered number four

Something switched like a latch that ignited the dusk into night and back to daybreak but got stuck somewhere in between. I cannot quite recall the broken sunshine or waking up but, due to my bare feet soaking in the dew of a new mourning, I hold the evidence of the waking that never really came. And now, over these nights and days and tides and full moons, I am emptied and holding still waiting for an explanation of this stark void that keeps me here.

"It won't be long now," she told me one night in her kitchen. "I know." Was all I could let fumble through my lips. She sat, rooted in her chair on wheels, her back bent and her head resting on the counter. "I know." And I put my head in her lap as I sat fetal next to her on the worn linoleum floor at midnight. Her hand now stroking my hair. It was autumn, 2013 and Montauks were still blooming in the front yard.

her tiny body falls to

the floor

in hopes of

catching the

sliver of light

escaping from

the hallway

and into

her room.

i live my life

a parallel of extremes

where babies nap

quiet still for

the single engine plane

arriving

safe harbor from the

block island sound

where dogs bark at

shifting pines

and

alarms offer an end

to sudden silence

the babies wake from

engine noise.

(for A.O.)
1999-2017

cold morning coffee isolated

by the bagged lunch you forgot to take

as you hurried to meet another day

of living and breathing

of learning and longing

to remain invincible.

one last kiss atop my

unbrushed hair and a

pit stop hug given from the boy

who called back love and mother.

forgive me.

remember me.

forgive me.

i love you.

forgive me this last time.

unconditional.

son.

please don't take me away

with flashing lights

and

sirens speeding

weaving HELP

through traffic

and

red lights.

rather

whisper well to my soul

softly

in the cool and subtle

sunshine rising.

mixing evening

with light.

remember a kiss on my

tired brow

and

i shall be released then

into the arms of

the One

who loved me first.

few things were left

behind

in the combustible

commotion of

gavels pounding and

paper signing.

among the

    voices

    and

    words

    and

    promises

    made empty,

    i wrote my name

    and walked away.

this next storm will

kill them

for sure

as the mixed,

maniacal march

roars through

the hesitant spring

to bring

the destruction of

the daffodils.

i meant

to sit

by your

bedside

but

the montauks

were dying

and the

soil

needed tilling.

i didn't

look at

her face

the morning

she looked

away towards

the far

edge of

the jagged

bluff that

called her,

come home.

her scars were real but the

disguise between the two were

almost incomprehensible.

with thorn and berries

staining and cutting her arms and legs,

the small girl offered her humble harvest

to the woman waiting in the yard with a switch.

with

   a

  requiem

      on

     her

lips

she

  holds

    the

      mended

  word

as

  the

    holy

      of

        holies.

liquid

air

seeps

seductively

upon

wilted

daisies

raised

by

a

dead

woman's

memory

pleading and pausing,

he wafts through antiquated memories

that entwine his smoke filled hair and singed footsteps.

quiet, now.

your skeleton key rattles in your pocket and

the flames lick at your silken coat.

and in the midst of the hurricane

she stood with her arms wide open as if

to embrace the foolish stranger who had overstayed its welcome.

spinning madly and screaming out the echoes of her past

bravely rooting herself as the rain and wind spat at her face and arms.

her feet were bare and toes curled, implanted into the sea grass that whipped her legs bloody

stopping to call out the inconvenient demons that

flew through the storm and laid claim at the very edge.

she had beaconed herself.

She stood.

dizzily spitting back the undisclosed warnings of a madwoman and yet recoiled her spirit

so it would not

be lost

to the sea forever.

each attempt to step i

slip onto

    the

        next

           tier

              that may or may not be leveled

              in what I am trying to attempt

              as i bind my eyes in the dark

        silence

        of

    9 past 12

to nothing by to go or have

to guess where my foot will fall

or collapse my restless body whole

HOLD

next so that you may catch me

in a quest to rescue.

i slip.

her eyes are such a

serene shade of green

when they cry

from too much of

a day gone wrong

and

violent shots

fire from the

soul in

such a panic that

her heart races for breath

she stands

in the rain

of april.

a time of surrender

her green eyes close and

face grows hot in the

shame of her weakness.

cement life and

gravel thought

drifting off into

black skies of spring

will but hope

only for the faint

music

of hearing

peepers

by the railroad tracks.

she's learned to look

to the

third floor windows

for signs of

life seeking life

from this gypsy traveler who

at one time

had her

roots planted deep

in the mire of her

memory.

her own third floor window

that shone her face

to the streets

below that

there was once

life

beyond this pain

and glass.

i see her dying again

the old lady

without enough

sun

she has wilted

after her glorious

december

struggling in the

scatterings of

april and may.

she is dying again until

 next time

when she will call

remember me?

i have been planted

in a pot too small

for my roots

to wander and

water does not renew.

remember me?

i see her dying again

and wonder if it is from

a longing for winter and

intrepid fear of the year

ahead.

there are no hands to hold

so i just watch

and wait

for the unknowing and

uncertain

refrain.

i see her dying again.

By the kitchen door, there were wicker baskets to cradle the chicken eggs

buckets hung from the rafters which needed to be filled by sleepy goats.

Opa's gentle hand would hold hers as they walked out into the back pasture,

stopping on the way to identify the trees and wildflowers

he knew by name.

screen

wet

scent

pretends

to

be

summer

while

the

radiator

hisses

in

the

corner.

i think of you now

as the sun sets at eight

in your railroad pajamas

wondering

where you'll go.

i close my eyes and

trace your face

the phantom boy

i have not met.

wondering

when you'll come.

wondering.

wondering

wandering

son.

(spoken word)

you sit there gaping at the statistics projected on the wall of your power point and power suite not knowing that i am sitting in the last row wondering how long it would take for me to dissolve into the ground and become one with the earth and never know how many people are here in this sanctuary i'm trying to make sense of something they have no idea how to comprehend. these people pretending to want to learn the disease depression and dissatisfaction of having a life gone wrong. gone sideways. gone upside down. i am here i am listening i am shaking my head and biting my cheek so hard they bleed but if i open my mouth nothing will come out but blood stained words i never got to say. the unknown phrases that race around my head and do not let me sleep until night has fallen hard and swift. do you hear me pastor? i am fallen fallen like the night but still, please look at your statistics and teach from your notes where you will never know the third girl in the third row. as i sit in my last row holding myself bolted to the chair so i don't get up and run. i have razors in my pocket deep that i promised i would put away and hide and never touch but can't find anything softer than the placement of my thighs and arms and nothing seems right for me to fit them in and hide them. i'm sorry i disappointed you. i didn't know what else to do. you cannot feel what i feel so please don't pretend that you do again referencing your power point with your power pointer and power suite. i am not a statistic. i am here i am sitting in front of you i am part of your baptismal church and i know jesus loves me i just wish he was here sitting with me in this room of propaganda and contempt for another world we haven't seen that seems so freely to spill from my veins and onto the floor where i can scoop it up and place it in a bag. i will not take my own life if that is what you are worried about i will not leave my children and husband alone without someone to weed the garden and feed the dogs and smile and smile and smile and nod and say please and thank you for not burying me yet but i am still a voice that has not been heard and i cannot return to the child i was before eleven and thirty-nine. it doesn't seem right my wondering what to do next or how to proceed or how to move on from the stones in my own pockets and candles that have been lit to offer a sacrifice for my soul because it sits in that bag. the bag on the floor. the bag i cannot even carry anymore. i am not sure. i am not sure what to do or who to call i stare blankly at your screen and wonder if you can hear me scream from within my soul just look at me and hear my voice before i am leaving. my head is too heavy from too much conducting and my hands are not steady from too much caffeine and too much empty air i have swallowed and allowed into my brain. i can not call you. i do not know what to call you except, "home" and that has already been sold at auction along with all of what is left of who. i. am. complete.

and this is how it goes.

oddly shaken from distant slumber so shallow and cool

begging my head to be kissed by cool lips and touched by cool hands.

i grasp the edges of the cotton blanket and rock

back and forth and back and forth until i am completely numb

expect for the lull.

my body aches from the toss and turn but i inhale the cool and

feel it in my belly like ice in a

vodka on the rocks.

the lulling sound of the fan in the window that blows in air, night air.

cool against on my body.

please let this shallow be deep enough to bury my racing thoughts that

prohibit sleep.

oh sweet sleep from rattling.

on and on and on and…

i am worn.

i am no longer aware of the temperature that

heals me.

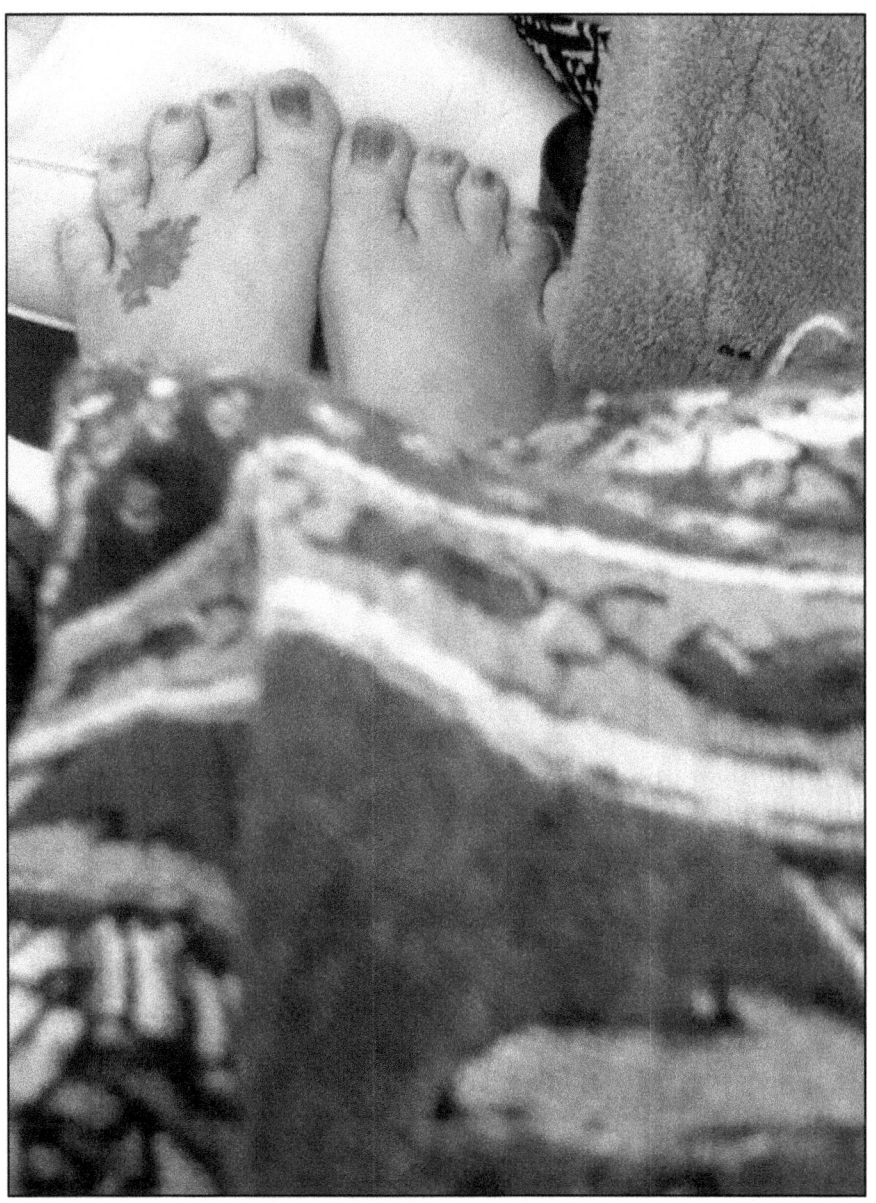

fleetings of her perfume linger

as she sweeps through the kitchen

and

through the hall of

time transcending time

of another woman who bore her scent

no one really wants

four year old frozen blackberries

or

a

dead woman's pillow

but

nonetheless

still they sit

in my ice box

and

beneath my head

destined to be a writer through

suicide and rage the girl who sat in

the back of the class examining every

page of nonsense that poured from

unknown sources pointing her to the

unknown voices tapping her fingers

and bouncing her knee

she never wandered totally from the tournament

from danger that so surrounded her.

the writer

and poet

the suicide rager

i don't see many sunsets lately

but not for the reason you may think.

my eyes are not dim and

my heart has not stopped searching

for that one thing that

brings closure

to a worn and fragile woman

but instead

i sing soft lullabies to babies

whose smiles shame the most

vivacious sun setting

those soft kisses

close my eyes

and gently float us all past the

dusk

and into the dark.

where we wait until

the

new, thin sun seeps through the nursery

illuminating the angel faces who are

almost ready to wake.

the well went dry in 77 when

the grass was frosted in the october night.

the island chill and foghorn noise arose from

the bluffs and

through the house with no insulation.

she carried me so my feet stayed dry and

stole the water

from the sleeping neighbors who

forgot to shut off

the outside shower.

the water was cold but we got out quick

wrapped in terrycloth and eider down

held close to her chest.

she hurried us back through the

stars and sea grass

to the home that was hers

on cold october nights.

fresh water and

earth dirt

scented

through the marsh and

bird sanctuary where

houses are built on stilts

by

old men

in waders

and

sun hats

shouting at the

motorcycle noise

speeding over

the cut through bridge.

slow down.

breathe it in, boy.

autumn is coming.

autumn is over and

the ambient air

of sour milk

and rotting apples

wafts from the

old mill built and

bewildered by

time and disrepair.

i'd walk you through

but the boards creak

danger

to all who enter.

the lost.

the passed.

and

the bees and

field mice have

mangled through the

support beams

of

childhood memories

and

fresh

pressed

cider.

i would like to feel better by

thanksgiving

instead of just counting the

seconds until

sleep

but

is there really a

timeline on

mourning

with seasons

swaying and pushing their

greedy way

though four years of

watching the

canadian geese fly

franticly over the pear trees?

four years of numb

and nothing to rest my hand on.

i am tired.

mournfully, soulfully tired.

i would like to feel better by

thanksgiving

my timeline is ticking.

she is often lost.

and it is impossible to

follow her gaze

through

tunnels of

dark pines and briar

where moss roams

north and dark and soft.

she unpacks there

her

october memories

recollections of holding

a dead woman's body.

startled only when the

monarch sifts through

the buddleja davidii.

she is often

so often

lost.

my mother will be dead tomorrow

which one would assume

by now

i would have grown accustomed to

the heart of the moment that

has silenced all the clocks.

four years now.

time to move on, you say and

why the hell are you

so

sad all the time?

snap out of it.

regroup.

replenish.

you have so many responsibilities

that do not require your

forlorn pitiful self.

smile, you say.

but really was it 4 years ago?

4 moments ago?

forever ago?

1,460 days

when the room was dark and

i sat by your bed and

you called *me,*

"moher."

i spoke of love and

permission.

i'll be ok. we love you.

i love you i love you i love you.

let me hold your hand when you are ready.

let me be the last voice you hear.

let me carry you

wipe your brow

caress my face with yours.

tears mixed with sweat.

you close your eyes and

i wait until morning when I stop

the pendulums from lying

and lie next to you until

time starts again and

you are taken from my arms.

my mother will be dead tomorrow.

i should be more ready.

(for E.K.)

bare feet on

bare pavement

from early november rain

leaves stuck like stickers

glued to the earth

balmy breeze in

old

red

oaks

and maple trees

peculiar times

the fifth day

of when

you were born.

nine moths

this day

given away the

lost children of

an inconvenient time.

left alone in a

stranger's home

waking in a room unknown

to their tiny blurred eyes

blinking.

when do the moments

the memories begin

of small feet on

solid ground.

easy now.

you are home.

thanksgiving.

these hands

once small

held tightly to yours

feeling your fingers like

security and

forever

we walked together

you and i

as the sun slipped down

and made its way

around and around

each new moment

spinning into beautiful bliss.

and now

this moment i am forever

a monument of where i began

and where i am bound.

and through you

i find myself

a man whose hands are strong

and perfectly fitted in yours.

holding tightly

feeling your fingers like

security and

forever.

her words tumble

out like

weeds

turned wild

from sap and root

entwined and

tangled

moving and slipping

clumsily grasping

the lamplight bedside

for blackberries and

bibles.

notes scribbled on

secret sabbath

pausing only

to dip her pen.

she begins again

tumbling.

why the struggle,

sister

in rolling your carpets

to watch them unfurl

serpentine staring

into subliminal

silence

you

push and pull

uncertain of the

angle.

position is everything.

struggle

quiet voice

whisper past my ears.

listening.

The field mice are at it again

the electrical wires have been chewed

and

discarded

leaving the old house on

lake quinsigamond

dark and abandoned

except for the young mother

and

her infant crying

safety solace someplace warm.

february howls

and

shakes the shutters

leaving her to wonder

if there is really someone knocking.

saving, helping.

peace in the snow.

(for E.K.)

19 christmases

past

and today

i put my girl on

an airplane

high

she left today

to grab

her

fire flight

and

her passion light

the brass ring

from childhood

shined new today

in the sky

you've jammed things up again,

stupid girl

with your tragic

words and life

unfurled

don't you know

that you're only

a speck

caught on glass that

 mires the view

of undone stones in

mossy places?

whose life comes from

being so dark?

do not look closely.

stupid girl.

your eyes will blind.

it makes me nervous when she's gone quiet

lost again in some dark place where only she can see

unraveling the here and past

intertwined with no real sense of

tides or phases of the moon or time.

it makes me nervous when she's gone quiet

her eyes fixed on something silent no one else can see

hearing the chatter of children and catching the

scent of wildflowers

crafted into crowns of forget-me-nots.

forget me not.

it makes me nervous when she's gone quiet

on the last sunday of the last year

clamoring, shattering, fighting the wilding within.

she folds her hands and keeps them in her lap.

she's gone quiet again and

it makes me nervous.

she keeps

seashells

in a jar and

counts them

upon occasion

just to be sure

none have gone

missing.

her hands were never the kind of

frail

that you think of with old age

or blue moons.

they were solid and strong and

able to write her own name

even if labored and thought tasking.

her hands were never the kind of

frail

you think of in accordance with

suffering sickness.

 they were soft and comfortable

even while grieving the last time she

held mine and walked

unfettered on the sand.

her hands were never the kind of

frail

that you think of with old age.

sixty-five year's worth of

work and sewing and

mending the souls who came

to mourn the night.

and tonight

I am awake and tired and wishing you

hallowed birthday on the first

full moon of your seventieth solstice.

never frail.

(for R.R.)

you sat on my porch

the day your daddy

passed from life to there.

hopscotch on the sidewalk

and ring around the rosie.

games of innocence and

all the moments before.

catching the ice cream truck

and skipping in the street.

your small hands not yet

mourning the grip of his.

you rest your head and

lean in for shelter

after too much play.

your mother will be here soon.

rest, child.

these are the last moments.

cluttered windowsills of

winter fixed and

unmoved in the

january freeze

recorded lows

forecasted in the

fist and fury of

new england

 ice and wind

and nor'easter wild

not intended to reconcile with

the prospect of a softer summer

when the sills will be cleared

and the windows will be opened.

she was the gentle

after the thaw

of frozen steps

and icy birch

that hung heavy

under the weight

of another winter's

echo

too solid and still and cold

unrelenting anger

until the ground

grows soft again

after the snow.

(for H.M. bonus daughter)

her summer wild in

sunshine autumn

she blew into

our lives forever

settling gently

through the

season's tides.

miles from the ocean and

confused by the

fog of december,

the gulls gather on

rooftops

to

welcome the storm.

(For Boppa)
(1917-1998)

It was cold but your

soft eyes gazed

and

tender hands

cupped my own

the last night she sang.

today,

in the snow,

i can still feel

their warmth.

the dead live on my street

(if only for a couple of days).

they spend their time only

eight houses down and the

living come out to see them.

the black suited men

come in cars and

line up in the cold just

to catch a glimpse

and offer

forgiveness

and scatter

lost secrets

that will fall

on

deaf

ears.

the timing was off and

the balance was wrong

or

maybe even something

altogether unfastened

that made her steadiness

of step begin to catch.

the black hands of the

the clock ticking

    ticking

        ticking

against

the bare white wall of

blank indifference

swinging as she goes.

this february morning

we wrapped you in a baby blanket

combed of soft cotton.

your preferred resting place.

and held you one last time

after your mighty cry signaled

your passing.

your arms reached out

and your eyes of amber gazed at

the distance

that does not here exist.

the ground is frozen except for

the garden dampened by leaves that

were never displaced, rendering it tender

for the spade to dig the grave of a

feline friend who once was content

to sleep on my pillow.

race track dredged

around the house

past rhododendrons

by retired racing dogs.

father sits on the stairs and

drinks his beers hooting

his cheers and gambles

as the greyhounds go

round and around

chasing

the rumor

that The Lady has

made them chicken

and

their bowl

awaits them

around the bend.

had my window been

closed

on

the sixteenth

day of

february,

i would never have heard

the eleven

canadian geese

honking

across the

rainy winter sky.

or the church bells that

chimed 4'oclock.

it's your birthday

said, mother.

february spring

the rain is still cold

while snowdrop flowers

push through the earth

proving all is not frozen

while the red winged

blackbirds hush silence

in the marsh to listen for

the squawking migration

home

canadian geese fly

over the hay field

through the fog

all the while

my hands are still cold.

her words were disconnected

from her thoughts and

 rearranged

in some garble

that didn't quite make

sense to her

let alone to the

confused listener

trying so hard

to understand

the

ramble flowing

from her

tongue and mouth

which

seemed to baffle

the frightened ears

who had

 already

stopped

listening.

i cried today

because

i had no money

to afford you

the circus.

you mocked me

at sixteen

because

you had no interest

and

you had already

seen the show.

i stopped by the

side of the road

to prune

bittersweet

for your grave

knowing full well

(all too well)

they would

be buried in

tomorrow's

snowstorm.

i can't find my shoes

which,

at this point,

would only be a

hindrance anyway.

(for F.S.)
(1894-1982)

the dining room was

always dark with

the curtains pulled

shut

to keep the winter out

and delinquent sunshine

from escaping the parlor

where the old man

with white hair

indulged the child of

his grandchild

with sanka coffee

and

royals

raspberry candy.

auf Wiedersehen, opa.

we never said goodbye.

she prefers it this way

floating above her

borrowed life

submerged in an

amniotic state

girded by the ominous

undertones of

a minor key performing

like a symphony that

was never written

and will never

be composed.

she just glides between the

here and there

never fully under the

the intent of being absent.

she prefers it this way.

(for E.)

cold, march, spring night

and your small hands search

for stars within

the silver strands of my hair

 and

the curve of my face.

your breath on my neck

and heat of your body

arching inward against mine

at bedtime

prayers and songs .

your humming vibration against

 my cheek.

these moments are fleeting.

your small hands on my face.

i will not forget the

cold march spring

the starlings have

come back to nest

but

the winter was

not kind and

left

nothing

in place

for their

home.

witnesses have

noticed that

she has

gone off the rails

to which

she responds

that they have

been invisible

for

quite some

time now.

big dog pup

untethered

and

chasing the

leftover leaves of

autumn's last frost

his boy tucked

under a baseball cap

strumming a new tune

in the sun

for the dog

to dance

weary

by after

noon,

the sun

emerged

shining

and

melted

the

morning snow

when the white gulls

raced in place of

the storm

and i met a

red haired

baby with no

socks or shoes.

spring in

new england

is

confusing.

she is not well today

(which is not unlike

most days)

barefoot in april snow

feeding the birds

and dusting off

daffodils

denying the day

when stopped very still

she could hear

the earth call her name.

she is not well today

standing barefoot in

the april snow.

she was beautiful

once when

the earth was

soft

and the children

were small

when fountains

flowed

from within

her soul

she was beautiful

to the unbreakable

gazing at the sun

unable to feel its heat

when dusk

settled upon her

feet

she was beautiful.

She was beautiful

once.

old men on

ocean rocks

feeble in the

knees

standing tall

on captain's watch

the ships start rolling in.

fishing pole and fairytale,

he'll sell you either one

but never believe he stands

out there for

victory

and

not

for

fun.

i let the happy in

today

the sliver of light

split in two

the dark of years

and

judgment and truth

it swarmed around me

like bees to a hive

then dove inside

hoping to rest

somewhere to hide

i knew not what to

make of it

it took me by surprise

this feel of happy

sunshine sky

this hidden life came

in today

sorrow hidden

in disguise.

milk weed

and

black bird

a slit of red to

count between

the stalks of

marsh and

barren trees

left angry after

this

new england

winter.

freckles on my

forehead from

a day in

the sun

a new silver strand

when it's come

undone.

crisp cotton sheets

blown dry by

the wind

a warm

bath with bubbles

to end the night in.

her hand upon mine

we watch the moon rise

i wait for her sleep and

praise Him

for this time.

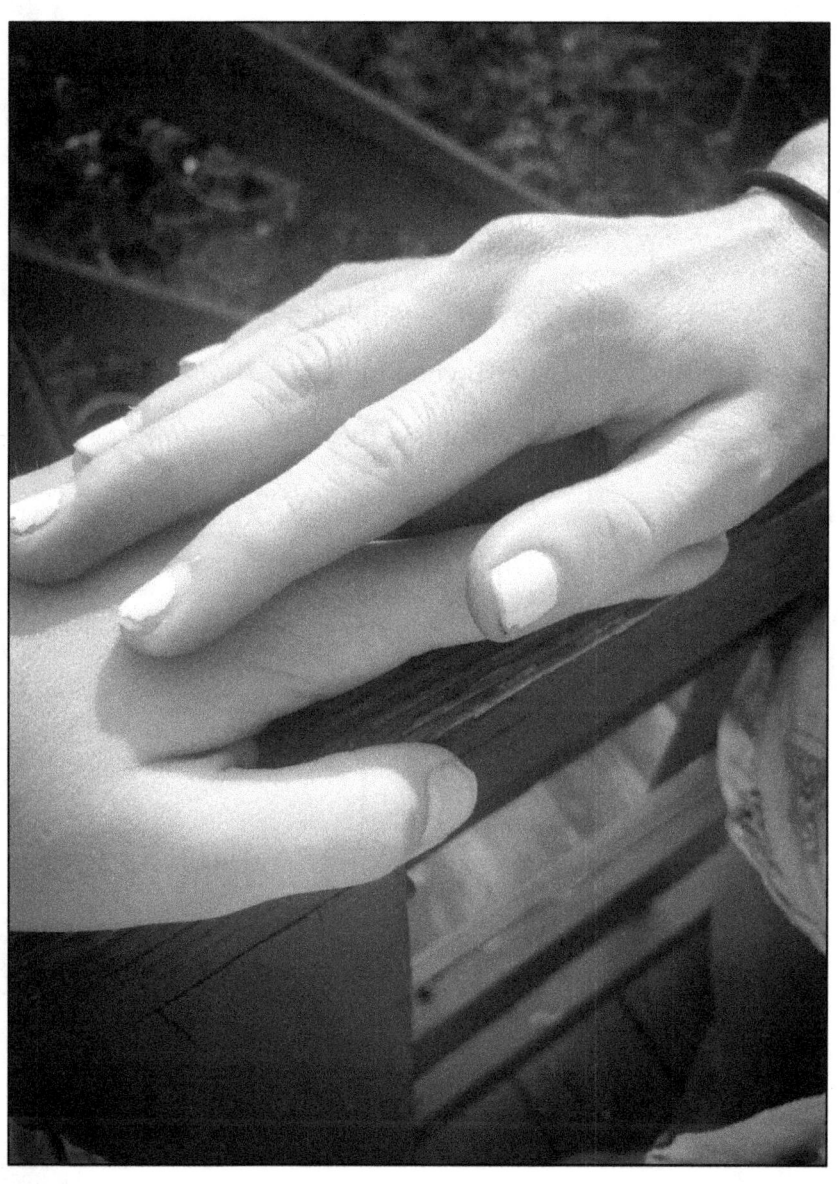

when the

coolness of winter

still lingers in

the hallways

grasping,

finding shelter and

bereavement in the

hard wood planks

creaking on the

second day of may

while the

heat of sudden summer

grazes

my breast like

a stray bullet

fired from a

nonexistent spring,

i move closer to

the window

in hopes of

remembering

what day it is.

she looks at me

and

i am whole

her hand in

mine

her entwined soul

within my heart

but not of my

womb.

she breathes

hot breath on

my face and cheek

and

traces the lines of

my face and hands.

all the while

the world is

happening

but

not for us

searching the

moon…

Peace

tonight

goodnight

dead

black cat

stranded by the

side of the

off ramp

green grass has

begun to form

his silhouette

i wonder if

anyone thought to

look for him

the day

he went to

wander.

what were you thinking

is something that

never came to his mind

when he left them gasping

 and

grasping for

steel hooks

on which to

hang their

high end

self imposed

gold dust dignity

of shameless

senseless

mediocrity.

he never thought

they would have

second guessed his

goings on and

goings out

but

they did and

  it stunned his soul like

lightening striking

his last four leaf clover.

she had no boundaries

really

her knees bruised from

praying

and her hands weak from

healing

the world that

could not be

saved

from what she knew

was injustice and it

infuriated her heart so

that it raced off of

cliffs and

rooftops and

mountains

drowning in oceans

rescuing those

who could not swim or

stay afloat.

her shoulders heavy with

burdens of bystanders who

said nothing but

"you can't save the world"

and shook their heads and

walked away from the girl

crying out,

"please,

just save me."

she sits,

her raven shawl over

tight, bent shoulders

feet in the cold sand

salt air squinting the

sting in her eyes

that have been

searching the sea through

the fog and crash and crest

ebb and flow

riptides and currents

tossing seaweed masses

roving like a wild

sea beast that

will not find rest

in the circumstances of

defeated fishermen

casting their lines in

the calming rage of

tide coming in

all around her,

she feels the decompression

of lightning in her veins and thunder

demanding her attention.

she can be found

hiding under

the bed with the dog

in the dark alongside the

skeletons that have escaped

from her closet and

rattle her breaking

soul.

each time,

pieces go missing

unable to be glued or

fixed or filled.

the decompression,

almost forcing her to

breathe between inhale and

out

with no instructions and

never knowing what comes next.

(for J.D.)

my heart is heavy literally from

the upside down gravity and

pulley systems of my

soul that have

gone in for repair due to

another malfunction of

mistrust and the

misperception of what

is real and what was a

predetermination of your

initial touch.

i've forgotten the

general pleasantries of our

official introduction.

i was much younger then.

the day I went into hiding.

the jagged journey which

began with the

gravity of a

single

first kiss.

some day, we'll go on a trip

just you and me

on our flying saucer ship

yes, some day, some day soon

we'll take a ride to the big

blue moon

where we will dine on

cheese and grapes and send

smoke signals for

all of

love's sake.

i think of my mother

from time to time

her hands like my

grandfather's and

eyes just

like mine

she comes in and out

through windows and

doors

through the tide of the

ocean my

children explore

on nights such as these,

i hear her voice sing

through crashing of waves and

rustling night leaves

snowy tree cricket and

traces of traces of

paths gone grown over

with thorns

and blackberries

still

warm from the thicket

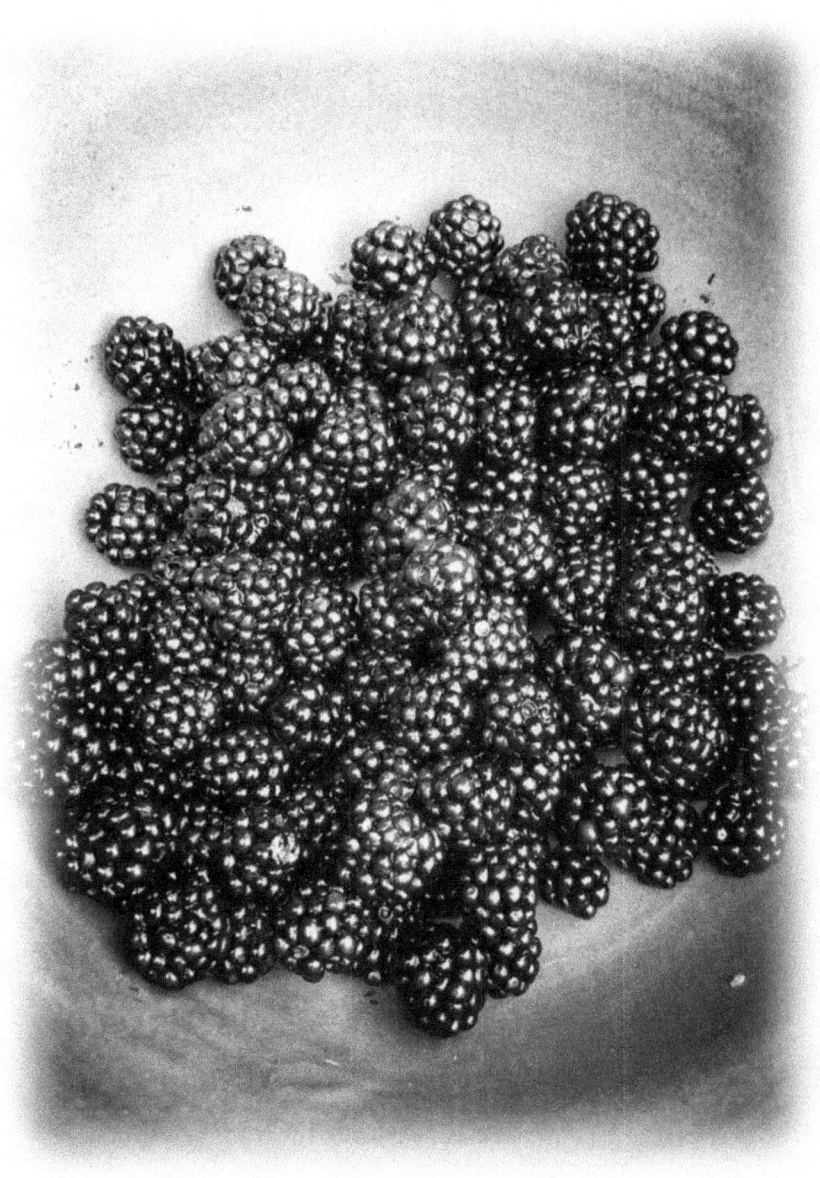

(june 2018)

i would like to say that

behind her

crooked smile

the one she depends on for

pretending that the air is not

strangling her very

voice from screaming in the

night for

someone

 to hear her when

she can't even find the

right vocal chords or breath

or strength

or anything, anything in the

darkness that has

developed like a

canyon around her with voices

calling from miles away.

voices as clear as day but

not clear as in this moment where

she finds herself alone.

eyes closed.

room spinning.

catching her breath

and wondering, wondering,

spinning, wondering

if this was the last time

and whether or not

her husband has a

clean shirt for tomorrow.

driving through the

darkened night of

eclipsed

moon

and ocean tides

i am yet to linger

heavy and full beyond

the veil of gauze and fog

your face the clouds,

voice and space

this darkened sky

full blood moon.

remember now.

remember now the salty spray

of tears which rose from an

ocean's grave

the grave that hides the day

not mine

reduce the light within the eye.

i am yet to linger

and set my pace.

steady and treading

tonight's tidewater

this full

july eclipse.

the men with mowers hadn't

noticed

through the tall and sharp

bladed steel and

grass the small

nest

almost abandoned

except for one who stayed

behind to stand his ground

he thumps the earth

beware

beware

beware.

good gracious

good night

i'm gonna

put up a

fight

for those rights I have but

oh, so few

these days are shared

with the voices of

you

believing in and

shouting my name

Hello World.

It's just me.

i've come to

see.

you see?

there are burn marks on the

linoleum floor from

her falling asleep in

the wheelchair

wedged between

the counter

the pie safe

the back door where

she spent the hours after

the house went to sleep

to smoke the

last cigarettes in the

crumpled cellophane

package.

I was woken by my

mother's voice this morning

and in that moment

 between

sleep and awake

my eyes quickly opened to

a brand new day

of her

being dead.

(for R.F.)

"they said it was cancer"

is all he let slip

as easy and plainly as

shifting through

 mail

accumulated

by the door.

they will burn my

insides with

radiation to keep me

alive, he said.

i guess we'll give it a try.

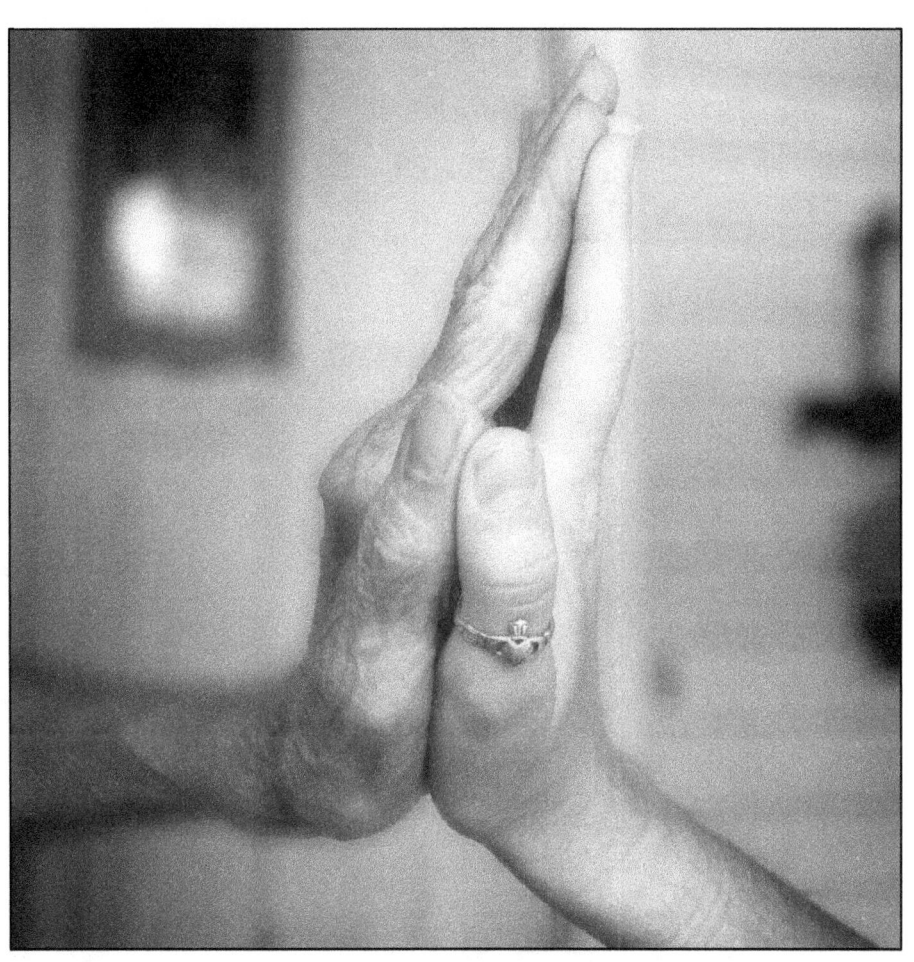

august evening

rushing past

across the road that

meets the marsh

heavy laden with flooded

fresh water

pre autumn night and

hay fields in the dark

jupiter balances beside

the moon

she smiles her

amber golden red

the rush of the moment

train racing along

summer exhales

it's almost time for sleep.

the drugs had

worn off and

everything was

crooked and

somewhat slipping through

the tiny spaces between

her fingers where she

tried to grip the

cemented solace that

seemed so suddenly

out of place

the matriarchs are falling

silent to the ground like

barren birches losing their

footing in

high winds and

hurricanes

coming up

revival through

compound and

rocky paths with

soft sand beside it

offering a

safe place to rest.

i am nothing but a

self-fulfilling prophecy

my mother's mother

her mother

before me

invisible and falling

silent to the ground

you'll know me when

you see me

the naked girl in

the back of the room

with

tight fisted hands

wringing the

weight away

shifting feet from

right to left

 in hopes they will

find a way to

run or

walk or

stand without

wandering away in the

clouded thinking of

what words will

come out

when she says,

this is me.

how do you know

when the root

has died

when the life has

surrendered from

not enough

water

sunlight

or

tender pruning?

when is it the

moment where

there is no more

unwilting of

crumpled leaves?

you can always try,

(i guess)

to reconstruct but

the root

will never be the same.

fists tight,

i perch the

top of the stair

with my bare feet and

toes curled around the edges

avidly wondering

if i can fly

there is

nothing so

spectacular

than

earth's first

offerings of black

red

raspberries

sun warm

new

from wild roots

escaping the boundaries of

a well meaning fence.

(for E.E.)

september sky

mired by autumn haze

obstructing the gaze between

me and it

while the operatic moon sings

sonnets of shifting planets

red to the right

the hush of night falls

streaming through

to the other side

of

black in a black ink sky

the singular solo to be

remembered,

applauded and

be

praised

(for S.E.)

poetry of joy and laughter

escaped from my soul and

released the light from the dark of my day.

you were born and the universe shifted,

spun

and

danced,

pirouettes in agreement that

someone had come

and the world

would never be the same.

sweet child of my heart

as if you were mine,

your mother's child,

my love is yours.

come dine with me on

peppermint tea

upon the rocky

galilee

we'll skip and shout then

pour it out

and ring the bells and tambourine

come with me out to

the shore

and cast our sins forevermore

we wave goodnight

engulf the light

have no regrets…

remember me.

Eulogy

I am my mother's only child. And although I hold that bond in the center of my soul, I would be remiss to think that it was a full proof statement. How many of you can attest to her love for you? The times you came to her home, knocked on her door, called on the phone. The times you reached out to find *hers* was the only tender hand reaching back? The moments she made you laugh or the times she calmed your tears and fears and offered comfort and solace.

She was so much my than just "Beth's" mom. She went beyond all measure to give you…yes, you all, the very best parts of her. Please, take comfort in that for she loved you and was always on your side. "Mother." How many of you can claim her? As you search yourself, I know that each of us were blessed enough to have been "mothered by her."

Now, being her daughter, I was exposed to some pretty awesome stuff. Stuff you just can't make up. As a child, my little playmates would come over and admire the "old family pictures" on my dresser. They would say things like "your grandpa and grandma look really nice and who is that one? Your father?" …and then i would have to explain that no, it was not a picture of my grandfather. It was a picture of a poet named Robert Frost and no, it wasn't an heirloom picture of my grandmother but of another poet, Emily Dickinson. And the man in the framed picture? No, not my father but Bob Dylan. My mother began early, you see. She had to. There was too much to teach and so many mountains of love to climb.

With me nestled in close, feet pajamas, and my mother's sweet voice, she would read to me.

Charlotte's Web was our favorite, e.e. cummings and the adventures of Paddington Bear. Together we would become lost in her love for language and words and sounds and the divine perfume of the yellowed pages of a very old book.

Through her, I lived the stories of her own youth and they were grafted in to who I am. I know of Cuttings Cottages and secret picnics in the Southeast Lighthouse. I know of red winged blackbirds, sea turtles and monarch butterflies. I know the ocean and ebb and flow of each memory of Block Island…a place she loved. A place she missed.

Yes. She raised me. Because of her, I know the difference between golden rod and tansy, the difference between real sea glass and "not yet ready" sea glass. I know bayberries and blackberries, brown eyed susans and Montauk daisies. I even know what it is to keep a shovel in the trunk at all times- because you never quite knew what wildflower you would see on the side of the road.

I recall an evening when I was a teenager and a "mission" my mother set out to conquer. Around 10 p.m. and with the shovel in the trunk, she and I drove to an abandoned property and if you tilted your head and strained your neck, you could see a patch of wild tiger lilies. Yes. She had these targeted for days. But I guess to a police officer, two women with a shovel , romping through an abandoned lot at night looked suspicious. I was mortified. But she simply showed him the lilies and explained to him that they needed more sun and she had a perfect spot in her garden and…..the policeman took the shovel from my mother, dug up her lilies, placed them and us safely back in our car and sent us on our way. 25 years later, those same lilies still grow in her garden.

Oh, she was so brave! Never afraid to take in a stray animal, a stray person, a retired greyhound or a lost soul. She loved so deeply and so unconditionally that you couldn't help but be drawn in by her warm smile and her example of God's grace. Oh, yes…she loved DEEPLY. She loved recklessly and loved forever. Hers was not a one-time connection but a life long journey she chose to take with you.

I am anxious for you to remember who my mother was. For those of you who knew her for her entire life and for those of you who came along in the later years. She was not a woman to be defined by her illness or her suffering. Instead, she fought it with every bit of her being. Her warrior spirit cheering us all on, she kept us smiling, laughing, dancing and rejoicing. Every day giving of herself without hesitation or expectation. Please remember her this way. Full of life and a simplistic joy which she so easily shared.

I would like to leave you with some of her own words-her own memories and her own poetic remembrances of her grandchildren…

She wrote:

"We play-you wear little red sneakers and I wear orthopedic shoes. I am the Queen of the land of Lemon Ladies. We mount our harlequin horses and their hoof beats are muffled by the wet sand and the waves that crest the ocean shores beneath an imaginary tide. Alongside us, run the queen's greyhound. We stop and pounce as if we are one spirit when we spy a perfect moonstone. I collect them in my brown velvet hat with the white rose attached to the brim.

When you later appear behind the potted plant, I see you have the table set for three black bears, a hippo, a calico cat and a very green frog. There's room for us, of course. Let us pour the raspberry tea and enjoy our very fabulous tea party. We had ordered lemon ladies. Grandmothers are never too old to play. Pass the cookies, my sweetheart, child of my child. Lemon Ladies are my favorite.

You are wonderful and you are Princess Hannah of Grace.

Around and again, your wooden pony circles to the music in search of the brass ring. You catch it in your hand and we both laugh. You, your pony and the brass ring charm me as if I were beside you on a mystical steed.

The tide is low at noon as we wade between the rocks and reeds-our toes wiggle in the salty silt in search of clams to collect in our basket to bring home to steam until they open and become a feast that I remember from a long time passing- when another island was plentiful from the sea.

We sit in the summer bright and hold our breath in the sunshine. I am the child within the child who wears my earrings from 1965 that now dangle under

your little summer hat-my granddaughter, Emily.
You hide-I'll seek my youth through your laughter."

THAT is my mother. My mentor. My father's beloved and my children's nonnie. That is your friend, your sister's daughter and a beautiful piece of your history that will be remembered when the full moon shines and the leaves fall gently from the Autumn sky.

About the Author

 Elisabeth King earned a BA in education and English language and literature from Gordon College. While a student at Gordon, she had the incredible opportunity to spend time closely studying English poets and poetry as she toured England, Cambridge, Stratford, York, Scotland, and the Lakes District. Ms. King then spent many years educating children, first as an elementary school educator and later a middle school English teacher. Currently, she lives her life by the ocean in New England with her husband, Michael and four daughters: Emily, Hannah, Erika and Bella. It is here, in the small town of Westerly, where she draws inspiration for much of her writing. This is her first publication through Stillwater River Publications.

Contact Elisabeth at www.rabbitholewriting.com **or** www.facebook.com/rabbitholewriting

www.ingramcontent.com/pod-product-compliance
Lightning Source LLC
Chambersburg PA
CBHW060032180426
43196CB00045B/2530